DOUBLE HELIX

by Barri Armitage

Washington Writers' Publishing House
Washington, D.C.

My thanks to the editors of the following publications in which a number of these poems, some in earlier versions, first appeared: *The Augusta Spectator*, "A Time for Blooming"; *The Bridge*, "A Time to Cast Away," "The Finish Line," "Gathering," "Marks," "Misery and Company," "Schooling," "Settling"; *The Devil's Millhopper*, "The Cake," "The Gardener" (previously published with the title, "On the Death of Our Daughter"); *The Georgia Review*, "Family Tree," "Fitting," "Replay," "Square Dance"; *Lip Service*, "Rush Hour"; *The Ohio Review*, "After Words"; *Paintbrush*, "The Bouquet"; *Passager*, "Dance"; *Poet Lore*, "Funeral Pilgrimage"; *Poetry*, "Double Helix," "Fall Ritual," "Self-portrait," "Trading on Gravity," "Weights"; *Prairie Schooner*, "Bedding Down," "*Journal*: Outliving Our Firstborn." Reprinted from *Prairie Schooner* by permission of the University of Nebraska Press. Copyright 1992 by the University of Nebraska Press; *Sand Hills: The Augusta College Literary Magazine*, "Measuring," "The Potter from Stoke-on-Trent"; *Southern Poetry Review*, "And a Time to Keep"; *Washington Review*, "Seven Loaves and a Few Small Fish"

The following poems have been reprinted:
"After Words," "Fall Ritual," "The Finish Line," "Misery and Company" in *Out of Season*, *The Amagansett Press*; "Family Tree" in *Carnegie Mellon Magazine*; "Self-portrait" in *Anthology of Magazine Verse and Yearbook of American Poetry, 1986-1988* "Square Dance" in *American Squaredance Magazine* and *Anthology of Magazine Verse and Yearbook of American Poetry, 1985*; "Trading on Gravity" in *Business in Literature*, Georgia State University Press

Publication of this book is possible thanks to grants from the Max and Victoria Dreyfus Foundation, the Jenny McKean Moore Fund for Writers, and the Prince Charitable Trusts, as well as donations from the many Friends of Washington Writers' Publishing House. It was funded in part by the D.C. Commission on the Arts and the National Endowment for the Arts.

Printed in the United States of America.

Library of Congress Cataloging-in-Publication Data
Armitage, Barri, 1937-
Double helix / by Barri Armitage.
p. cm.
ISBN 0-931846-42-0
I. Title.
PS3651.R4663D68 1993
811'.54–dc20 93-7012
CIP

WASHINGTON WRITERS' PUBLISHING HOUSE P.O. Box 15271 Washington, DC 20003

For Dave, David Jr. and Alice,
and in memory of Nancy

Contents

III

The Gardener

knows his trade, knows how to choose
the thickest stems from stringers, knows
the right reasons for pruning down to ugly stubs
poking up six inches from the ground. He knows
the stalks will stand all night as if remembering
over and over the feel of the saw
as each cut brought sap to the surface,
will stand in the cold night not cold enough
for frost, as if trying to remember
the new bloom, shape that will soften,
juice that will thicken—the good enough
reasons for the mass of dead brush whirling
and writhing at the edge of the dream.
He knows roots will reach into well-worked soil
and returns before dawn to smooth again
the sealer, clear and sticky, on the wounds.

I

Just as we can smell something
only when it begins to evaporate,
we can taste something only
when it begins to dissolve. . . .

—Diane Ackerman
from *A Natural History of the Senses*

Square Dance

Blue-checked cotton made
to match, we court
and fluff like cranes.
Hip to hip we swing,
your eyes the pivot
for which there is no call.
In time, a change so gradual
I barely hear the moving
to another key—the words
that skip us on to split
the ring, to separate
and take the outside track,
circle up four until I stand,
birdie in the cage, pulled
to the grand right and left
by hands that slip on past.
"Gentlemen, walk single—
ladies, back to back—
remember your man as he comes
around the bend."
Costumes and bodies blur
until your face brings a lift of song—
the feel of the bones of your back,
arms circling me home,
swinging me round and round—
layers of slip lifting from my legs,
the two of us slowing the pace,
swinging the pure spin seen
from space—blue earth
banded with drifts of white.

Double Helix

I. GIFTS

1

At thirteen, you passed me
notes—scrawled and folded tight—
then searched for answers
slipped into cracks of our desks. Later
in dance class, you stood with the red-eared boys
lined up at the gym wall. Soon I felt
the sweat of your hand. When the bell rang,
the hours unwound like hair let loose from braids,
and I opened my arms to gather
books with your name spilling over the margins.
Outside, spring rains inched the first crocuses
from the ground. One by one they climbed
until the whole yard was spotted purple and gold.
You brought me a red-cupped tulip that year,
and in science we saw pictures of ovaries
loaded with 400,000 cells. We learned even space
isn't empty: light and sound stream out,
wasted, waiting to be used.

2

Twenty-one, and a riot of color
brimmed from a small diamond
as we walked the profusion of fields,
bluebonnets and violets pressed and carefully laid
on our unsteady scale.
The mouth, the hands, always wanted more.
One summer, as the grass gave back its green
and my body swelled with the heat,
night after night you felt the new heart's beating.
Finally, we counted ten fingers and toes.
For weeks you kept pace with me
as morning came early to your drawn face,
and I could hear, as if for the first time,
the clang of Father stoking the furnace
before my feet touched the cold floor—
could see Mother dozing by a fever-soaked bed.
We bared our selves layer by layer,
sometimes raw, yet the steady tide of our gifts
brought me coral, then jade, then gold
to dangle from my ears or circle my neck.

3

Past fifty now, and the fall air droops
with the distant rumble of rain, drenches us
in the near scent of peaches—still good—
as men harvest bushels before the trees
give back their leaves. Along the path,
we stoop to dandelion fluff, blow seeds
and laugh as in the old photos.
I arrange bittersweet to add color
to the house, pot amaryllis for the winter.
Our shelves bulge with sweaters and books
as gift options narrow like arteries,
but sometimes you bring me perfume
from flowers picked in their prime,
and tonight I'll make you
honeycake that keeps a week.
When the widow shared her food
with Elijah, it lasted through the drought—
lately it seems, the more I bake,
the more the oil rises in the jar.

II. STAR ATTRACTION

> "Our senses grab only a little of reality; the eye takes in a trillionth of the energy which reaches it."
>
> —Robert Ornstein and David Sobel
> *The Healing Brain*

1

Just married, we shared our bedroom wall
with a pair whose tempers blared each night.
Fridays the climax would come—
the high voice baiting, *Show me you love me*—
sometimes the crash of a dish,
a bass rumble finally entering, then silence.
We'd step out for air, looking up
as patterns and myths circled
like foxes in tail-chasing stoles.
Back in our room, I'd roll
a towel for the draft at the door
and pull out the daybed. We'd dive
for the center without turning back the quilt.
That year I learned the cracks
of the bathroom tile, the bulge
of the linoleum, each mole on your back.
Sometimes the ache of fullness. Sometimes
a fight, and I'd sit at the window to wait
for the first star, for desire's slow rise to begin again.

2

The next-door couple moved on,
sent a postcard of L.A. at night—
spirals of color brightening
hospitals and dark corners of the city.
"Can't seem to live together," she wrote,
"but I'm only alive when he comes
back, and we try it again." We stood
on our wooden balcony, the stars flickering
like images moving from a projector's wheel
long after the actors have gone.
With the turning of time, we tested
the light from our own windows, walked
at dusk watching other lamps glow
as moves left scattered behind us
carpets scrubbed to the wall, a son's
playhouse, and pots of flowers overflowing
from a daughter's death.

3

Tonight, papers strewn like patchwork
on the bed, you read to me of two stars
discovered locked in gravity's embrace:
a white dwarf, collapsing
under its own weight, sucked
at the circling neutron mass, stirred
high tides that spewed out
rays of matter to pound
the surface of the caved-in star
with explosions, ton after ton.
Through the blackened sky we cannot hear
worlds dying with spectacular light,
only the quiet—filtering down
from the room I remember again
as we look out to winter stars
lighting a trail as pale as Gretel's crumbs.
The silence reaches deeper than breath
as you lean over me
to pull the shade.

Self-portrait

For Dave

Eyes, covered by thick glass, disguise the two,
four, a thousand parents who passed the blue
recessive gene by blue-hot touches in between
mending the plow or stirring the beans.

Mouth tries to perfect a closed design,
lips stretching since high school trying to hide
teeth that fought for space in a too-small chin
and practiced for hours natural grins.

Skin smooths over the face, guards a world
of feelings that pull and push to be heard:
of blood that rushes when the covers slip
when you take off my glasses, press open my lips.

Family Tree

For my father, 87

I

Your voice doesn't miss a beat
as we keep these hours at your borrowed
hospital bed, and you tell again
the begats you've studied for forty years:
"Thomas Allison, he left England in 1662
for a thousand acres near Mattawoman Creek,
now called Thomas Creek, running east and north
from a marked oak by the riverside
to a marked oak by a marsh. His first wife
had Charles who left the land but passed
the line to us." Now you drift
into sleep, circadian rhythms lost
in the delving of longer and longer naps.
Once you drove me deep into that land.
A few large stones leaned on each other,
surrounded by smaller graves. You lifted me
over a wire fence. I copied you
as our fingers pushed into worn holes,
one letter at a time.

II

Downstairs next to the coal bin, you stored
the copies of deeds and wills,
a box for each family branch—
in the first, the father who left
before you were five. Seven years later
your mother died, ice-packed with pneumonia.
I don't ask if you search for that boy
left crying on the black apron
of your grandmother's lap. Later you worked two jobs
and survived like a scraggly plant—

tough enough for life on a slickrock wall,
blooming from May to July. I remember you dancing
with Mother those summers when I was a child
until breathless and giggling she begged you
to stop, and I tried to hold onto your knees
as we all spun like Mayflies
until we dropped.

III

When you wake, there's time for a walk. I pull
the brake on the wheelchair, steady you
sinking down, eyes at child's level.
Outside on the asphalt path,
insect shells crunch under my feet.
Winged seeds scatter everywhere.
You point to tiny maples, perfectly formed,
springing up under the trees.
We pass feet, legs, belts.
Suddenly, I'm a girl standing up
on a chair and you're shining
my best shoes for church—the clean smell
lasting longer than shine. Tell me again
of Thomas and Mary his bride, of the son
who survived and the land and the oaks
no longer marked. Tell me again.
I want to get it straight.

The Potter from Stoke-On-Trent

For Thomas Barry Gotham, Sr.

Grandfather, stub-fingered potter,
we tour to share the English sky you left—
silver-blue, cloudy as the swirled vase
you brought on the boat to Ohio.
"Grandfather's best," Dad would say,
placing it high on a shelf above the couch,
untouchable as fire.

Now in a shop thatched like a fairy tale,
I scan the Wedgewood—rows of flat-eyed blue.
Shelf after shelf of cookie-dough molds
cling to boxes and candlesticks:
white-robed Greeks under quiet trees,
white butterflies caught on hidden pins,
circles of olive leaves drained of green.

I push past clipped smiles
to the brush at the edge of the Trent.
The ripples move as slowly as your hands
shaping clay to the wheel,
stretching the lips,
smoothing the curve at the neck.

Funeral Pilgrimage

For Great-aunt Anna (1876-1978)

I

I buy my way from Augusta to Akron.
Before the flight, they X-ray my granola
and thermos of juice, peer into you,
find the tumor that bloated you pregnant.
They feel my hips for guns, examine you on all fronts
through your open gown. The one-way ramp,
a determined bed that carried you, lifts me
to the plane. I learn there is no way out
except through approved exits.

The flight attendant tells how to keep safe,
shows a mask to help our breathing near the end.
The engines rev. I fight the forward thrust.
Past a hundred, then a hundred and one,
almost a hundred and two. Somewhere in those miles
you lost yourself in the steady moving,
laid your head back, gave in
as I do now.

I look down at the shag carpet of trees,
the mosaic of turquoise oases.
Cars crawl like the years you gathered us
to the smell of turkey and shoo fly pie.
I see all the sand traps now:
red doodles of Georgia clay
branching like skeletons
slashed and dug out, ready for more dust.

At dark, lightning appears in the peepholes.
The pilot assures us it is far from our path.
Below, patches of dots move closer—a last moment
before going under ether. Lights become
a blue runway. A roar, a jolt as I resist
the sudden slowing down.

The pilot says I can go.

II

I meet my gray-curled parents, your last brother Walt.
We follow signs down the speckled tile of the terminal
past miniature TV's, twenty minutes to the coin;
past shops of wicker, mugs, and gyroscopes.
A child points—"Plane." Anna, *you* were plain—
your mother's German jowls and chin.
They tell me how you screamed for her at the end.

At the church, I pick up a card:
Anna Susanna Carolina Oswald Wise.
Words settle over your closed face.
As the caravan rides to the grave,
this time you lead the string of cars.
More words lower you next to Uncle Wilk.

We go again to *Yanko's* for spaghetti, fill up
on stories. When we came for your hundredth,
we'd called a waiter to open a stuck window,
turned back to find you'd done it.

You slipped me your golden locket that day—
you corseted, Uncle Wilk in stripes.
As a child, I asked if you ever kissed.

We linger over a photograph:
you and six others squeezed in,
squinting, your dress eerie with age.
The middle of your face was always old.
On the back you've scribbled,
"Part of the gang—find me."

Marks

At Canyon de Chelly, Arizona

"For He knoweth our frame..."
Psalm 103:14

"Anasazi," ancient ones.
Your plastic bodies in the diorama,
white clay Rorshachs etched on the museum wall,
call me to the red cliffs. I pay the dues
and climb into the hot-seated deuce and a half
for the long bounce on the sand-tracked canyon floor.
John the guide says, "Yahtahey"—
hello, goodbye—and sometimes to a question,
"Wala"—I don't know. Bumping along
with fifteen other pilgrims,
I crane my neck to the top of your world:
Black Rock, Fortress Rock, Massacre Rock
jutting out like heads of beasts.
We pass shaggy cliffs, all colors of the sun
with purple shadows rippling in their clefts.

John tells us you lived when Crusaders
fought for land as dry as yours.
Here and there, footholds defy gravity
next to the stick men, arms and legs
stuck out like railroad signs,
the squiggles of lightning
reduced to your size. I find
a wedding legacy: one small pale hand
next to a larger, slapped on the red rock, high up.
Did he kiss her fingers
before he laid them in the wet clay slush
and pressed them to the canyon wall?

We chug to a stop.
A part of the ruin, I stand,
my chin pointing up to one-sided deer,
round women. Finally, I walk with the others
to the remains of your sandcastle,
count ten square-holed rooms
swept clean as a mortuary is clean,
without the flowers. Dust roils
on the steps to the kiva, burns
my eyes as we descend.

Wala.

Rush Hour

Mobile caves creep home,
edging from light to light.
I sense his stare in his rearview mirror.
Sleet swirls, locking us in.
I brake, start, brake in rhythm—
follow his slightest move,
careful not to touch.
Only our tracks merge.
Exhaust steams, brains idle,
thoughts slip out
through window cracks
and hover above each car
as shapes move close
under cover of dark and mist.

He pulls to a faster lane—
I shift, stay in line.
A Dodge fills the gap.
Turning right, headed for home,
I pick up speed as the snow
keeps splashing in whirls
before the wipers begin
each sweep.

A Time to Cast Away

Today I didn't tell you, Father.
You've given up enough already:
golf, some hearing, most sight,
the privacy of private parts.
The boy keeps skimming the surface,
your brain cleaning itself
as you talk of syrup on cornmeal mush.
Restraints at night keep you from a paper route
in the morning dark.

Protected by scarf, rubber gloves,
and mask, I took rags and broom to tackle
the dusty piles you'd moved over the years
from house to shed, honor to dishonor.
Insects had left their casts and zigzag trails
on folders of neatly filed tips: How to Hook
the Ball, How to Pick the Perfect Club.
Filling box after box for the heap
at the end of the drive, I thought—
I am my father's daughter. My files bulge
with clips on how to accept loss, make
every word count, fight stress.
The other day, I saved one about bodies—
sometimes just the head—being frozen
for later return.

In the shed I kept my resolve
through bags of practice balls, used
batteries, sweaters with holes, lopsided
shoes, and underwear stretched out of shape.

Since the Depression, you'd made sure
not to be caught short.
No letters or photographs from loves
that didn't last. In the corner,
some books dimpled with mold,
your name penned in the flap. I wrapped them
round and round with clean tissue
and laid them on a bare shelf.

By noon, foraging neighbors began to appear.
A woman on a three-wheeler bike filled up
her basket with bottles of turned wine,
a boy carried away six bags of insecticide,
an old man held up your rusty saw
and ran his thumb carefully
along the edge.

And a Time to Keep

Blue Willow with fine cracks on the white—
Grandmother's surprise for your wedding,
surviving fifty years, this box of dishes
filled over and over with meat or cakes.
When I was a child, I dried each piece
wondering if the blue boat would suddenly bend
and try to squeeze under the bridge.
The set moved toward me as time moves—
slowly, like your hand guiding mine
folding eggs into batter or shaping
cinnamon rolls. Mother, you fit
into one room now, so you shipped these
to me—stiff paper, no bows.

I unwrap the first plate, its rim thick
with a maze of symbols twined and curved
like yours and Father's fingers interlocked
in the bedside photo, a close-up of your rings.
Inside the circle, cobalt willows wave,
blown by opposing winds. A tree, top-heavy
with blue oranges, towers over the house,
the huge fruit growing like love let loose.
Chinese sweethearts, changed into swallows,
hover as if ready to kiss or collide.

Seven plates and cups, five saucers, a teapot
and creamer. Stacking the pieces by size,
I move in rhythm, unpacking faster and faster,
the gift just beyond the wrappings...

and see the lovers, wings like outstretched arms,
fly high above teahouse and fence—
a flutter just before they swoop, then soar,
sailing through the blue-edged band to discover
a sky bright with torches.

I push more wrappings aside and hold,
at the last, a covered serving bowl—
your back's permanent round
or your bending long ago as you held open
a small bottle of vanilla
for me to catch the smell.

Schooling

As David's plaid suitcase expands
to hold another cassette, I roll his socks
into small fists, trudge with my mother

up a first-grade hill, clutching a pouch
with sixty-four perfect crayons.   My hand
is clammy, hers sure as the steady pace.

By winter I'll skid and slip with laughing children
on the unshoveled slope, our mittens
clinging to branches and each other.

We've stripped the room, stuffed the car.
His hands sweat on the wheel
as we drive two hours of curves

to Whittaker Hall. Gripping his bag,
he tags after the girl
who leads the way to the dorm.

I follow my mother through heavy doors
that creak like castle gates, down giant halls
to a room full of inkwell desks.

The desk in the corner of his room
smells like printer's ink.
I trace initials carved in lopsided hearts.

He spreads sheets and tennis magazines
on the bare mattress, turns
to the girl with hair to her waist

and asks her name.

Settling

Before falling, snow forms in six-rayed crystals
around starters of clay dust or salt.

This morning skipped dawn, as if the sky
changed in a moment of grief from dark
to silver-white, while an overnight snow
draped flaws and upgraded the shoddy—
even the aging roof, shingles curled.
Home from college with his girlfriend's picture
in his wallet, my son's already loading
his camera, lacing his heaviest boots.

The snow seems to stretch out time, a watch
running slow, as we step into a world of flurries.
A bad day for burglars. Every mark freezes
as if cast in new cement: a stray dog's
trickled yellow dots, the zigzag claws of birds.
We duck the spray from the news truck
rumbling by, its tracks dragging dirt
to the surface like a tabloid's headlines.

Muffled sounds well, and then pack down with our steps.
At breakfast, we'd heard of a mother and daughter
trapped eight days under earthquake rubble:
Susanna Petrosyan unearthed a jar of jam
and fed it all to her four-year-old,
took off thick stockings to bundle the girl,
pricked her own fingers one at a time
to suckle the child back to life.

As David lives out his twenty-second year,
the age his sister reached, I feel her last winter,
her final spring come back in shifting layers.
He stretches to shake pillows of snow from a tree,
showering my hood with flakes. Never prepared,
I'm jolted by the trick photography—
her mouth blurring over his, her lips playing
at the corners just before his laugh.

We pass the last house and cross over Ward's Creek.
Along its ice-hung banks, each bright berry
stands out. I wait as he snaps photos of trees
dividing and reaching. Around me, it's a snow
long ago, and he's patting a three-tiered man,
storing him in the garage to make him last.

Then—we're back home, and snow suddenly stops
before noon. In an hour, the lawn's pitted
as scarred skin, the street a dingy slush.
I watch him trudge to the mailbox. As he retraces
his steps, an airmail letter slips to the ground,
no doubt from *the one.* He stoops to pick it up—
barely wet—and waves it in his glove-thick hand.

II

The rain won't be ice—
I won't sky-dive flip
to the bottom—won't crash
like a green chirping grasshopper...

Are there really brakes?

—FROM "GREEN LIGHTS ON A BICYCLE"
NANCY ARMITAGE

A Time for Blooming

Your sun-browned limbs have practiced
all the year.
Now, dressed carefully in white,
you wait the April light.

Dogwood—your skirt spins wide,
passers-by applaud your flawless dip,
a Dresden figurine.
What matter that the music box is set
a minute only for a pirouette?

Gathering

We should've called her Halley,
looping back after finals
to leave her traces—a glove
or sock for us to mail.
That last visit
she gave us a single candle
streaked with red and gold.
I smiled at her choice—
sturdy as cabbage stew,
thick as middle-aged spread,
that cylinder sat
in its wrought-iron base.
Yet it lifted
for her match as we came
to the table she'd laid out.

During that supper she tried to explain
recursions—"you build something
by assuming it already exists"—
lost us in math, art, and music,
a tangled fugue. We drifted
from mental to elemental:

How do you last
with four hours sleep?
her brother asked. "The body does
what it has to." Adapting
like viruses, her father said.

Or roaches, I added. "Even nitrogen
lasts. Ours could be Cleopatra's,
moving from lungs to earth
to the food on our plates."

As we lingered, the candle's flame
bent toward vacuums left
by our laughter and breath,
following us each by turns.
When she snuffed it,
whorling smoke turned to dust
too fine to be seen, joined
the forty pounds that settle
on the average house each year.

The school break over, her gift
became a half-burned bookend.
She returned to a window
lined with wine-bottle candles
melted to the quick. She'd forgotten
her Hofstadter, her *Eternal Golden Braid.*
I'd wrapped it for UPS return
that night we heard of her crash...

As the earth's shadow hollowed the moon
and fall gripped the last trees,
we drove to Elliot's Funeral Home.
Music followed us down the hall.

I made myself turn that corner.

After Words

All these days of her burying,
bits of well-meant chicken and fruit
stick in my throat—clumps of unsaid words
jumbled with those shouted long ago.
Once, grounded a week for coming in late,
she climbed out her window,
slept all night in a field.
                                        At supper,
her usual time to call, each chance
ring of the phone pulls me up like a puppet.
In dreams, I wade waist-deep in slurry, her voice
rising and falling ahead of me—an unmistakable print
on a sonograph.
                              Stories I've saved
fill my whole body. My mouth opens of itself,
begins to shape our secret jokes as if her head
would turn. Sometimes she's at her old desk,
dialing a toy telephone, each number
circling back. She stays on hold for hours
as I try to match an American phone
to a foreign plug, but thc cord hangs
slack.
          Last night the scene changed,
almost worth the wait for sleep—
four boys in the car that killed her
were chasing us. She outwitted them,
sneaking into a house and out the back.
While they searched the cellar, she jumped
on her bike, I held on behind. We sped down
a brambled path, chattering like schoolgirls,
knowing we had a lead.

Journal: Outliving Our Firstborn

Too late for sleep and too early
to rise, we turn to each other, two cords
intertwining. Sometimes his warmth seeps
through me as if passion could reach
far enough to heal. But often we lie
there, leaching remnants
of the days.
He opened our album
last evening, slammed it shut. Later
in the dark he spoke of the photo
from our hike up Mt. LeConte—we'd raced
when we saw an elevation sign, asked
a girl with a flowered headband
to snap us bunched in tight—one of the few
shots with the three of us.
My mind drifted
to blackbirds: one flew away, and the others
spread their wings to hide the space, chattering
as if to teach the fence how nine might add up
to ten—smart bankers shuffling assets,
relabeling loss—the way that dreams
restore the dead.
I felt him brace as I told
the one from yesterday: I was Nancy at a party,
crowded into a room at the wrong housc.
I kept searching the rug for my contact lens,
every loss more than itself, my fingers begging
the shag, raking through as if a path might lead
away from pain. Above me, strangers kept laughing

until I woke, hands covering
my ears.
I wrapped myself closer
inside the makeshift circle of his arms,
told him how I'd rummaged in that box
of clothes and tried again to wear
her denim vest.
She took nineteen hours
to arrive—Dave's stories, the sudden
rush, my insides heaving, her cry—
and only seconds to leave: a flash of headlights
miles from where we slept, false fire now
against the backdrop of night.
The hours rub
and blister. We drag our legs and arms apart,
put on clothes already laid out, slip into shoes
that feel like childhood's hand-me-downs,
swollen at the wrong places.

The Finish Line

At twelve, in a yellow slicker, she biked muddy fields,
pedaling against the sky's threat.

Nights, I return to the scar in the road, scrape
in the gravel, clutch a twisted footstrap
and a broken comb.

*

At two, she strained the springs of the rocking horse,
winning for hours in a private race.

Nights, she rides the edges of my headlights,
forward and back with the thrust of her legs,
music pushing from within.

*

Days, she sprawls in the police photo,
bike caved in like an old mare.

Nights, she moves ahead of me on borrowed light,
orange triangle strapped to the seat of her jeans,
her ten-speed poised to crash.

*

Tonight, I ride out my lights.

Bedding Down

I circle patches of graves and potted mums,
wind the borders to her fresh-cut stone.
Tracing her name, I picture her at four,
pretending sleep beneath the petaled garden
of grandmother's quilt. The corners of a grin
begin to play against the silence of her face
as she waits for me to tap her arm, magic godmother
bringing cocoa topped with cream.

I dig my fingernails into this soil.
It moves easily. My mind opens
the car's trunk, grabs any tool—
the tire wrench fits my hand.
Piling the rumpled grass,
I dredge through layers of clay,
tear off the crimped sheet to quiet her shivers,
massage her stiff arm until it wakes.

The Cake

Melting shavings of chocolate,
rich as leaves folded into earth—
my first time baking in the gray months
since the call that pierced our sleep,
since the sheet pulled over my own face.
We cleared your rented room, carted away
the iron skillets, the half-empty boxes
from the A & P—dry milk, brown sugar, rice—
then took a picture of the bare mattress
and the plastic bags stuffed
with books and quilts from the small chest.
I crack an egg on the edge of the spinning bowl—
the yellow dances, turns
into batter the color of mud.
We stood for that photo, holding
pieces we'd sorted from the wreck—
"debris" they called it at the scene.
We brought it all home, gave away your clothes,
lined up books on shelves, quilts on beds.
I reach for the canister and run out of sugar,
fill a cup with yours from the A & P—
a cup that measures a cup
if I don't pack too closely,
if I allow you to ride your bike into the night,
earphones playing you happy
until you're hit from behind,
tangled, and tossed into the November sky.
You lay in the night, stayed
flat on the ground as if you knew,
as if you knew the bowl would stop
and I'd lick the beaters,
salty and sweet. The baking goes on,
the pierce from the toothpick says
it is done...

The Bouquet

From the bay window, full as a garden,
I watch the driest winter yet,
the azalea, skinny as bone. Inside,
I move from plant to plant, water
until soil can take no more.
Last year the parade of florists—
Park, Blossom House, Holley's—
ended here at your window, Nancy.
Each carried tokens of green—
clay pots in baskets like hats
with satin ties.

When water has deepened channels
in clay and seeped like rot
through straw, I'll pick
the ribbons, a clutch
of color for spring.
I'll heap them in a bowl,
gather the days that are not, keep them
like bridal shower bows.
You would have called it a party,
pinned this red one in your hair.

Fall Ritual

Even the marigolds on my windowsill
speed on to seed, showing it's time
to shorten the path to earth.
You always stay at twenty-two,
you, the expert at shortcuts:
three cakes in one bowl,

four quilt squares, or eight, at a time.
Your bike, faster than cars at rush hour,
seemed almost welded to you,
sped you along the night's straight edge,
armlight blinking gold,
until a Chevy cut you short.

Outside, I soften a groove in the clay.
Maroon and gold petals, dry as confetti,
slip away at the slightest touch.
I wriggle the seeds apart
and push them into a common bed.
Reluctant to cover up,

I savor the feel of earth,
then sprinkle it, pack it like snow.
Bone of my bone, you were packed in me,
grew from meat I chewed, from milk I drank—
seed buried in seed
you carried to the ground.

When snow's patches have melted
and the flurry of birds returns
like the rush of rain,
I will kneel at this earth's pocket
as flesh of the springtime's flesh
begins to crown.

Replay

At breakfast we cover the night
with words we've spoken before.
They fall on the table, cards in solitaire.
Something calls from the bottom of the deck—
our daughter's voice, an echo three years dead,
each tone weaker by half. You'd dreamed again
of being in a dugout after a lost game—
you the pitcher, winding back the inning,
the wild ball meek in your hand,
arching over and over
a magnificent curve to the plate.

Last night the television glowed
as we watched the space team line up and leave.
Day after day, songs stick
in the throat. Some we try to erase,
but one we replay, as if this time
we could find the right groove
to lift us past the explosion filling our lungs
as smoke trails down, two fingers speaking slowly
a language for the deaf,
its words frozen on a mother's open mouth.
This morning we switch channels,
run back the tape to waves and smiles—
a home movie with hands shoveling food
from mouth to plate, the line of graduates
marching backwards up the stage.

Atoms shuffle in and out of us,
breathed by everyone on earth within three weeks.
Cells play out a kind of pattern dance—

stomach lining replaced in seven days,
skin in a month, liver in six weeks or less.
In five years, the whole body renewed.
Last night I dreamed Nancy watched again
as I laid out photographs—the ones of her
as woman, young girl, child—falling
in perfect order.

III

Many waters cannot quench love,
neither can floods drown it.

—FROM "SONG OF SOLOMON"

Dance

I speak of the wedding dance,
seeing only the whirl
of motion and color,
and your eyes
deepening,

speak of the allegro
spasm of discovery,
octave on octave crescendoing
until we beg
for breath,

speak of the lullaby,
you in striped pajamas
offering to pace alone
to calm the screeching bagpipes
of the night,

speak of cha-cha, choo-choo,
and Bingo was our name-o,
you in a red sombrero
down to your chinni-
chin-chin-o,

speak of missing a step,
of toes tramped,
of laughing—staccato and doubled up—
to the blare of bands
on Saturday nights,

speak of learning to march
to the beat of a dirge,
insistent, moving toward
stones lined up
in order of grief,

speak of trying a minuet
to the choir of children grown,
and you holding out to me
an armful of music, Victorian
only by cover,

speak of the long slow tango—
one leaning, then
the other, as lights begin
to slide:
                one shadow, perfected
by timing.

Weights

Like children split by divorce,
all items are stacked to the right or left.
The price of gravity forces the choice—
cotton balls move north with your job,
leftover Crisco stays with friends.
Movers with magic markers wrap the past
in brown paper. Grief I sorted
two years ago with our daughter's clothes
piles up with the boxes from her room.

We lie on the quilt left for the night.
Next to my head, in light from the bare window,
the holes of the phone-jack stare.
At the border of my dream, an alien slips north,
blood pounding. Land creaks and shifts
as a blindfolded woman balances scales.
A man at a desk rises, squeezes
a coffin back through the fence.

The streetlight goes off as sun begins.
We touch, heavy as lodestone.
Miles north, the rumble of a van
pulls out from a load-check, beams ahead,
tuned to a station picking up
love-cries that stretch like rays.

Convention

Never the same
flight since our daughter's death.
We play the odds, keeping one of us
for our son. This time I'm ahead of you.
Outside the Holiday's twelfth floor,
an air raid of flakes as I dial
to recheck your landing, an hour late.

The whirl of snow—
wings, seats, wheels—
hits walls and curbs
as figures walk backwards to the wind,
arms crooked over foreheads
as if warding off blows.
Shielding my eyes, I see
between my fingers, know your face
in the swirl that rushes
headlong to the ground.

A voice thanks me for calling United,
urges my holding on. I imagine
wires stretching toward dialers
all over the city, alone in rooms
or feeding quarters from booths—
"You will not be disconnected."

Thin music drags through the line.
I stretch the cord to the window,
watch snow falling over the hoods
of women and cars. Turning back,
I slide the phone to its cradle,
redial to hear again
such promises.

Dredging

We read together on the twilight patio—
A man and woman on a folk-art dish.
The garden compost crawls with living soil
While crickets work their music like a drill.
Newsweek reports a naked kidnapped child
Calling from the hole of a latrine;
Her mother says her screams now rise each night
Although the stench is gone, the trenchfoot healed.
Later that night, the story excavates
A sludge-covered fossil, half-submerged
Leviathan. It rises, stalks me through a maze—
But then—skin to skin we turn the key
To a twisted lock, rattle it, trying to take
The ending down another street before I wake.

Measuring

"According to a national survey on sexual desire,
men peak at nineteen, women at twice that."

The magazine blends with the buzz of meadow
in foothills warm with trillium and columbine.
You toss a frisbee, a red barometer
in the gusty air, as our son shouts
with the stretch of each catch.
Far off, I see the jagged horizon
leading to Clingman's Dome,
remember our first unspoken pull.
My stomach went into little crawls
at your voice, and I picked the lint
from your shirt, silly for the touch.

Too young those days for questionnaires,
I'd not have guessed the ledge we'd reach last night
after the washer overflowed. Muscles rippling like a rope,
you helped me mop, then grabbed my hand to climb,
dizzy for breath, above the timber line.

The Ultimate Harlequin Romance: Thirtieth Anniversary

I know, analogies break down.
But picture an ovum as Belle,
a dream of round perfection
hidden deep in a dungeon
behind those circular moats
and walls, a trick lock at the mouth
of an acidic river leading to her cell.
She doesn't flirt or throw roses,
yet she'll emerge to see her fantasy come true:
a troop of admirers swimming upstream to fight
and fall—for *her*.

Millions take a wrong turn, millions more
wilt in the current, whipped back by the gauntlet—
many-tendriled cilia guarding her banks.
She opens to her choice, closes
her walls forever: instant monogamy!
He drops his boyhood—vestigial tail—
and they begin. What dancing
and carrying on at their private party,
skinny-dipping in a warm pool, their senses
pushed to the wall. Over and over
they revel, echoing every trait of the other,
each pore brimming. Eight days of this delirium,
a honeymoon trip, until they decide
on a place to call their home.

Illusions, like babies waiting
to be born, must finally face the world.
You and I ride the twisting strands
of a double helix, slide down and tumble off,

our wind knocked out, then hold
to the rungs and hoist back up, pausing
to gather what can be salvaged before
the spiral begins its turn and we fall,
sometimes more heavily, sometimes
screaming or wearing black. Dulled,
we turn on each other or turn our backs,
then slowly circle to face again,
groping toward that first party,
senses reaching beyond sense, still learning
to ride out the story past the end.

Seven Loaves and a Few Small Fish

There's more than liquor I can't take straight.
TV for company, I cook: *Washington Today*
distances back-alley danger as medics give
blood to a youth stretched flat. When a woman
shoos small boys from the scene, one yells,
"Those were Uzis—bap, bap, bap."
                                                            Shots ricochet
later in dreamwork. I stand at the edge of a gorge
with a maze of street lights below, the surface
mirroring an underground that lengthens and curls
back on itself like toenails of the dead. My legs
buckle, too tired for the path winding downward
and through to the other side
                                                      where a mother
kneels by her dead son. The day's skin peels
further back. I feel the broken pavement cold
on my knees. The wet of birth-blood is sliding
down her legs, and she holds her son's slippery length
against her navel, his cord uncut. Someone
wraps him in a sheet.
                                            I wait with her all night;
we gaze at his closed eyes as if he were newborn.
We see him grow as a boy's body grows, hair
and muscle shaping each new stage. He pushes
like a plant through dry soil. She leans on me,
watching as if we could somehow stop the stem
from its gradual twist.
                                            The morning mail is a crowd
at my door. I give amnesty to one cause at a time,
including body parts: kidney, heart, and eye.
At work, they deduct for United Way. Pygmies,
orphans, whales. Rain forests. Refugees.
The blood of Abel spills. My left hand
watches my right hand writing checks.

Bracings

I

Something there is that doesn't love
the crooked: a plumb line tests
the mason's bricks, "Stand straight"
rings from mothers and sergeants,
bands drill, and surgeons rearrange—
yet the artist sets the crockery lid ajar,
rumples the blue-edged tablecloth,
and scatters a few grapes before painting
the life she longs to make more
than still. Nature finds room for randomness:
a leopard's spatter-painted dots,
the intricate veins on an old man's cheek,
the swill of waves—but whose hand draws
the line between curved and contorted,
beauty mark and mole?

When I opened my mouth to each new dentist,
his eyes would widen: "How about orthodontia?"
Still using the Depression's frugal scales,
my parents had always said, *No*. Later, my own
sparse budget helped me say the same,
and home I'd go to work on personality.
For years I lived with my mother's teeth
jammed into my father's narrow jaw—
through parties, interviews, a wedding—
then month after month in waiting
rooms, my face behind a magazine, while
braces straightened Nancy and David,
my own imperfect replicas.

II

The last child set free, extravagance tempted.
I hated my criss-crossed incisors—angled
oddly, splayed legs of a nervous child
onstage—yet hated worse to *pay* for pain,
and months of baby food. I tried to hear
my husband say he loved me anyway.
Forming a truce with my stubborn mouthmates,
I resolved to leave behind a skull
still grinning, smile askew,
an artist's delight.

Then, with age's gradual letting go, teeth
began to loosen, mocking childhood's
proud losses—no replacements underneath.
The latest dentist wiggled each, pointed out
on giant charts the dangers of "mobile."
My overbite, pitting upper against lower
for decades, must be stopped.

III

One month later, as my dentist came closer
holding a palette full of metal, I grabbed
his mirror, touched each of those crazy front teeth,
the smile my husband had married. I dreaded sharing
my mouth with gadgetry, but saw how wires
would gently prod, while bands around the molars,
deep-rooted pillars, resisted chaos.

Within days the shifting would begin, weakening
past bonds, harnessing the unseen force
that holds us together or pulls us apart,
taming it as the bride separates strands of hair,
drawing them smooth and winding a braid—
until love reaches out in the night,
and waves spring loose again.

Misery and Company

(for R. F.)

> *requiring our lives to have*
> *this permanent pull*
> —Roland Flint

The idea sounded good—reduce grief
by grouping it, divide by half, and half
again, to an eighth or even less, depending
on the number of Compassionate Friends
gathered in a room. Still, I couldn't face
their meetings. I only knew—in a moment
the clock could stop, and nothing
start its beating again.

Eight years gone now—
and today at the Writer's Center, a poet's reading
about his son pulled in me like stitches.
Afterwards, as I moved with the crowd toward wine
and cheese, words that politeness silenced rose
against my throat. Does he still awaken,
bones shivering, afraid to look, knowing
each night the slow spin of hands will pass
that time, an unblinking eye stamped
on the traffic report? And if he sleeps again,
do his dreams keep turning back to the sudden
news, when it didn't matter what to eat or wear—
yet choices that would last forever must be made:
what clothes for the child, what music?

I wanted to ask,
"How many children do you have?"—to see how he adds
or subtracts. I'd count out for him those times
I was *able* to intervene, inches from disaster:
a truck backing up, a loosened balcony rail.
I wanted to cry how I hate grief, yet sometimes
long to flaunt it, to tap the shoulder
of a stranger in the grocery as we pick over
apples or pears. And tell.

I waited in back, fearing the circles
a pebble can suddenly churn, then opened
his book to the poem I'd wept for
and walked in his direction.

Fitting

Bridesmaids, the five of us stand
in our slips, all ages and shapes showing,
waiting for her to drape the red silk,
let out the hips, take in
the cowl neck. The folds at the waist
will hide that tummy bulge, she whispers
from between her pins and lips.
Quietly bridled, we give ourselves
to her practiced eye, then shed the new chance
of each perfected dress.

In the closet, my wedding dress yellows.
This anniversary, one rose stood
for a dozen. Aspirin in the vase, and still
the bud stayed closed. I expected twice the life—
a week later buried it, shriveled and black,
under supper's chicken bones.

The calendar moves toward fall,
I stand in the rose-colored dress.
During the vows I hold my bouquet,
all shades of red, next to the bride's white orchids—
hand hers back after the bridegroom's kiss.
My tears don't come until you lay
your arm across me in the dark—
I'm singing and sewing my own white dress,
each day like crystal. It fits again,
and we dance, your spice-smell a meadow
with two young horses—far away.
The dress slips off, the music rises
like the smell of earth plowed for winter,
the tang of apples and sweet herbs,
the colts becoming one colt prancing.

Bedrock

I

We laughed at the story as we filled our own
lovers' jar—a *pebble* each time for a year—
enough to take them back, one by one, as passion
settled into the groundwork of our days.

Shifted by work, sometimes escaping it,
we started to gather tokens as lasting as earth.
Drawn to all that glittered, the two of us rummaged
at highway cuts, culling pyrite or lapis.
In the Tetons, we found a blue feldspar
flashing like a cat's eye, and partway up
Clingman's Dome a mountain-shaped quartz,
its crest translucent pink.

Restless, longing for more, we gleaned farther
fields—a loose chunk from the path leading up
to the Parthenon; pottery shards at Stoke-on-Trent;
a thumb-sized rock on a Spanish shore, embedded
with shells as delicate as gauze. One year we added
white pumice from Okinawa's cliffs: I waited
where the Japanese had jumped, surrendering only
to death; you spent three hours climbing down,
nursing your bad knee, to save one hole-pocked stone.

II

That first year, you'd shown me how rubbing
makes diamonds glow in the dark. Our thirtieth,
we hiked to an outcrop in the Alps. Far beneath
the valleys below, lava gathered still, ready
to burst from the inner bottle of earth—
most brilliant before beginning to cool.

Less in a rush to collect, we stood for a long time
tracing years of sediment exposed, thick layers
folded and melded with thin, crust arching up
against crust. Later in our room, the air
exuberant with chimes, we lay down
on sheets grown spare and pliable
from many washings.

Trading on Gravity

Voluntary or not, the pull
begins with the eyes.
At Livingstone's Lounge
in the changing light of the jukebox,
you draw me out to dance.

We marry, cart our groceries
and dressers up three flights.
Each morning we throw off blankets
and rise—boomerangs flying
out to others, back to bed.

Children add weight
or weightlessness. We kiss
scraped elbows and knees,
hike down Granger's Gorge,
join booster clubs.

Mirrors keep finding
more sags. We cheer
in concrete stadiums,
cross country, walk its edge
as surf tosses up, drags out.

Years tug at the balance,
news wears. We brace
teeth and foundations, pull
together, pull back, pull muscles.
Paint peels, fruit falls.

Earth covers our losses:
the great ones, boxed and buried;
the small, 100,000 pieces
a minute—flaking skin,
salt, saliva, lint.

Our donations increase:
more hair in the drain,
more sweat at tennis. But tonight
as I roll close, your touch makes again
the moment earth becomes air.

Kevin Pierce

Born in Columbus, Ohio, Barri Armitage grew up in Akron and attended Muskingum College (B.A.) and Syracuse University (M.A.). She has lived in Germany, New York, Hawaii, Georgia, and Maryland, teaching elementary grades, poetry in the schools, and adult basic education at various times. While in Georgia, she did graduate work in English at Augusta College and the University of South Carolina, and from 1980-1984 she was poetry editor for *The Augusta Spectator.* Armitage currently lives with her husband, Dave, in Silver Spring, Maryland.